23. June, 2016

For Andrew & Hais,
Thanks for your kind
and support.

MW00624924

WHiPStitcHES
RANDI WARD

*Dedicated
to the memory
of my grandparents*

CONTENTS

Doe

Starring
the soft
silt loam
with morning
at her heels.

At First Light

They lit out,
the white tips
of their bristling
tails bobbing
above
the bloodweed.

Morning Glory

Don't tear your dewy
lips kissing my muddy
boots; soon the morning
sun will sip the sky
from your mouth and turn
the world warm.

Good Shoes

"This world
and the next,"
she'd mumble
stubbornly
scrubbing the muck
from our splitting
soles.

Permanent

If I'd just let her
roll my head,
she said I could be
a pretty girl.

Creek

Decapitated
dandelions
don't disturb
the thirsty
cattle.

Buzzards

The black kettle
boils, churning
high above me
in the glare
of noon.

Pond

I reflect it all
with my evaporating
spirit of rain.

Water Hose

My terrible thirst
slurps hoses
to hissing
water moccasins.

Snake

Second nature
for you
to slough us off
between crumbling
cinder blocks.

Cattails

Mangy
cattails twitch—
a bullfrog
skitters off
ripples
of sunlight.

Wheelbarrow

A black feather
sinks
into the rusting
sunset
mosquitoes breed.

Gravel

Taillights
of today
skid-mark
my brain;
I spit
out the loose
gravel.

Lights Out

Fall asleep
before the bathwater
stops running—
you don't have a prayer.

Dam

Lonesome
lock whistles
never know
why
they're wailing
but blame the river.

Threshold

Blades
of butterfly
knives
blaze
the heart:
heat
lightning.

After Berry Picking

Your purpled fingers
braided
broad blades of orchard
grass into this crown
that makes me wear my wilting
brow high
in the canning heat.

Frog

Even this
wise frog
has probably
mistaken
a ditch
for a pond.

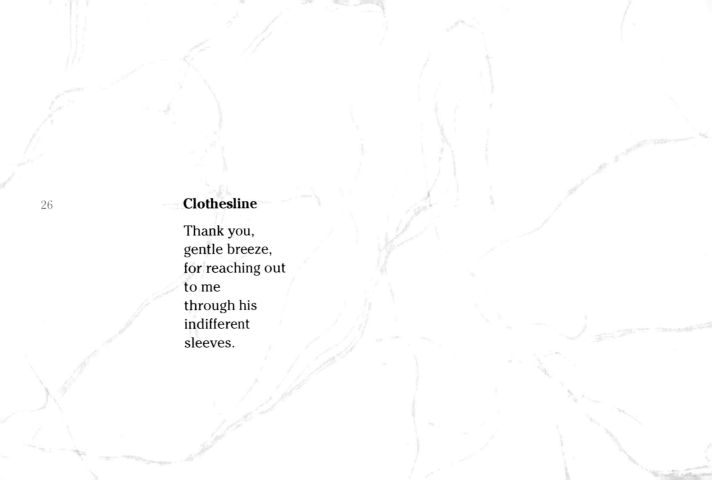

Clothesline

Thank you,
gentle breeze,
for reaching out
to me
through his
indifferent
sleeves.

Nest

Heart-shaped
hornets' nest
dangling
from a lichened limb—
stinging resentment.

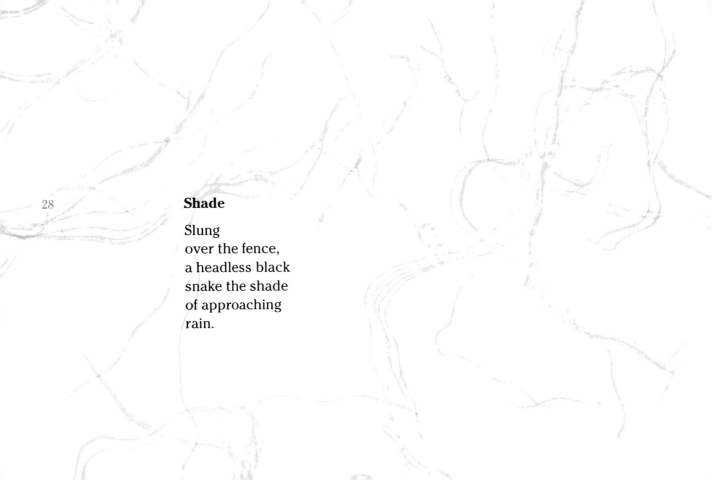

Shade

Slung
over the fence,
a headless black
snake the shade
of approaching
rain.

Lightning

Frantic silverfish
scurrying
between couches
of darkening
clouds.

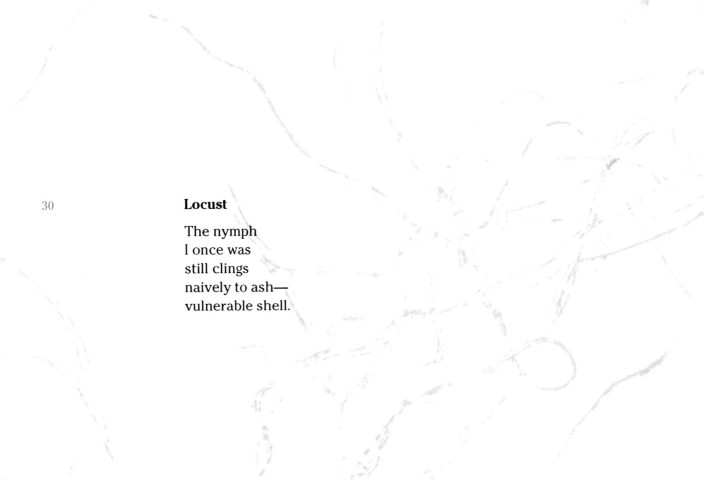

Locust

The nymph
I once was
still clings
naively to ash—
vulnerable shell.

Fence Post

Does the locust
post slip
farther downhill
because its wren
heart abandons it
each August?

Mother's Hair

Tangles
of torn stigmas
withering
at the edge
of the garden.

Galaxy

Constellations
of sawdust
matted in her
vast black
curls.

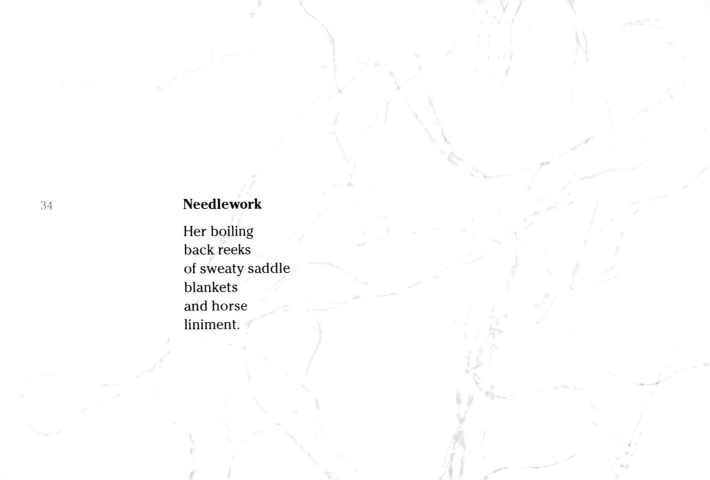

Needlework

Her boiling
back reeks
of sweaty saddle
blankets
and horse
liniment.

Bath

She soaks long
enough to make
a blind mirror cry
her deepest bruise
blue.

Fawn

Planted in
the tall timothy,
your dappled hide
took root and you dozed,
trusting
that she would return
before the mower
found you.

Second Cutting

By brittle bones,
we mow bright
waves of meadow
to gray moths.

Phone Call

Soon the stork
will swoop down
and snap me up,
because heaven's full
of better kids
waiting for my bones
to be born.

Rabbit

Everywhere
I rest
my head,
a caged rabbit
devours her
young.

Maze

Heaps of infested
blankets bristle
dark patterns
no one can escape.

Fleas

"It's all in your head,"
mock the fleas
crowding around
brimming sores
I've dug
raw for another
drink.

Mobile

Dirty clothes
dangle
above my groaning
bed
from the broken
light.

Door

Somehow,
fireflies
still find
ways to slip
through
the keyhole
and keep me.

Watch

Minutes
of meadow
voles told
by talons
gripping
a fence post.

Pond

I can't help
thinking
the pond is cloudy
because it's full
of snapping
turtles.

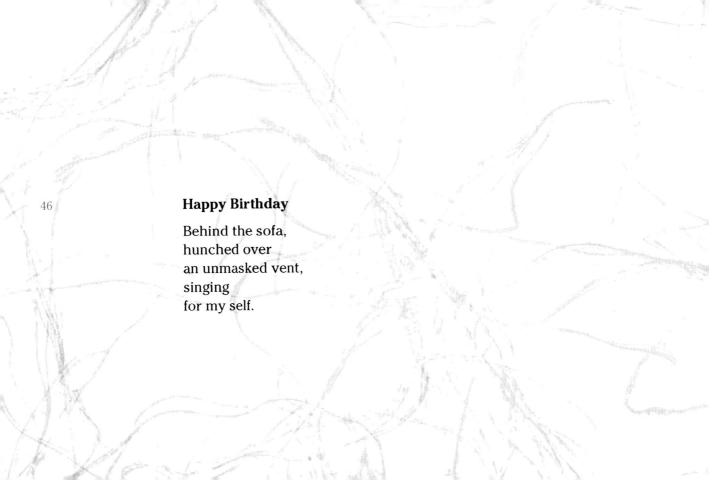

Happy Birthday

Behind the sofa,
hunched over
an unmasked vent,
singing
for my self.

Spider

We took turns
dropping rocks,
laughing
to see her young
scatter—
tiny sparks
doomed to darkness.

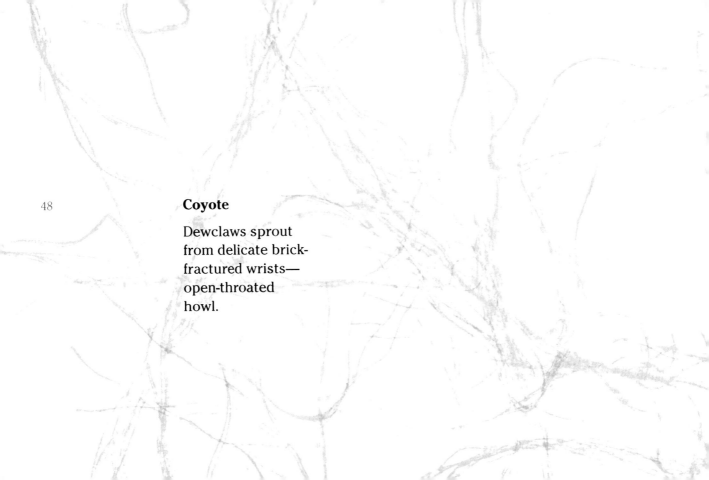

Coyote

Dewclaws sprout
from delicate brick-
fractured wrists—
open-throated
howl.

Brother

Sitting on cinder
block porch steps
taking potshots
at the moon.

Fiddling

Dragging
a dull saw
across the stob
of his head
till worms
surface.

PTSD

If raised
too quickly,
he'll think the spoon
in your hand
is a loaded gun.

Stitches

Eye to eye
with the patient
needle
stitching
my cheek
shut between
sniffles.

Tea Bag

How could
that little staple
inspire so many
hysterical hours?

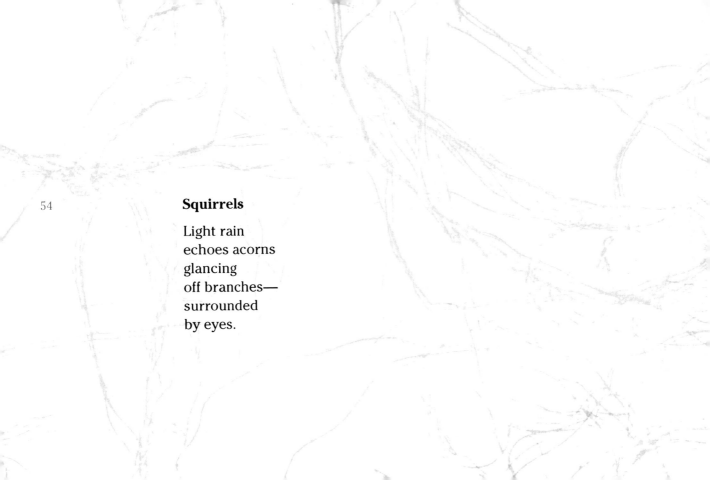

Squirrels

Light rain
echoes acorns
glancing
off branches—
surrounded
by eyes.

Combat

A whitetail
clearing
the fence
before he can
fire reminds him
he's dead.

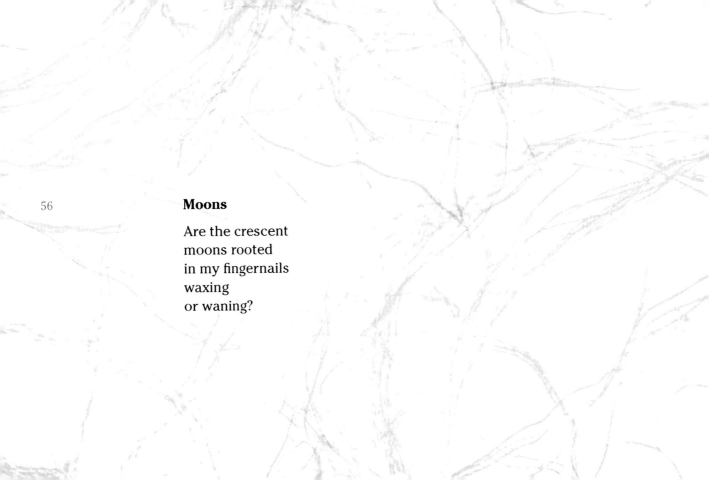

Moons

Are the crescent
moons rooted
in my fingernails
waxing
or waning?

Leaves

I sleep
with the smoke
of autumn leaves
smoldering
in my moon-damp
hair.

Skein

Awakened by gray
geese gracefully
unwinding
dawn's primrose
shadows.

Window

Fiddleheads
of frost fingered
by the morning
sun melting
my heart-
strings.

Hatchet

A hungry blade
bleeds its bite
away
by the gate—
hush
of wet snow.

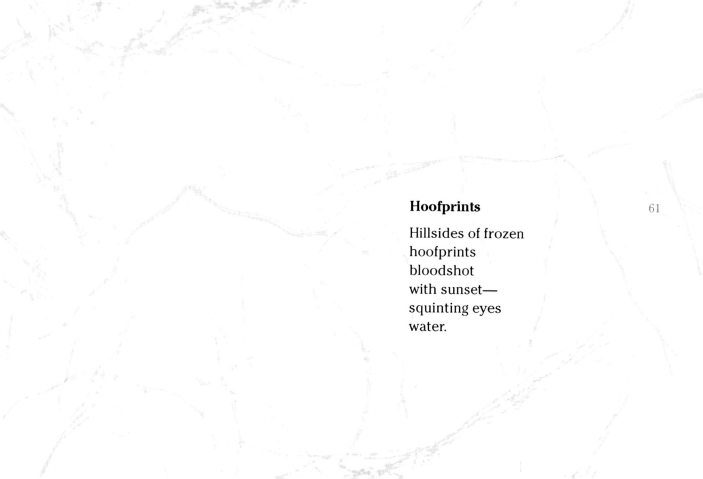

Hoofprints

Hillsides of frozen
hoofprints
bloodshot
with sunset—
squinting eyes
water.

Laying Up

There's death
in these dimples
vexing the knoll—
an arrow
to the bone
beads
a coverlet
of snow.

Cold Snap

Starving
by starlit
sycamores
silhouetting
the blanketed
ridge.

Skiff

Snowflakes fall
through withered
rustlings of red
oak leaves—
drifting
off to sleep.

Moon

All night long,
the moon's doomed
to bucket
after bucket
of drawn
darkness.

Foal

A blood bay,
a blaze
smothering
in its gray
horizon.

Afterbirth

Pacing and whining,
the dogs lick
their quivering
flews at the clank
of the shovel
scraping
the stall floor.

Pitchfork

Why
can't the cows see
this pitchfork's
the only thing
holding
the gate shut?

Broomsedge

Sweeping snowy
hillsides ablaze
at dusk—
my fingertips
burn.

Gate

Oh merciful
gate, break
these legs
for me
so I don't
have to walk
home.

Stray

To be
a black cat
in blue cold
waiting
for any door
to open.

Sycamore

Calm convalescence—
a sycamore's solitude
dissolving snowflakes.

Redbird

Have you
ever seen
a redbird
light
on a strand
of barbed wire
at dawn?

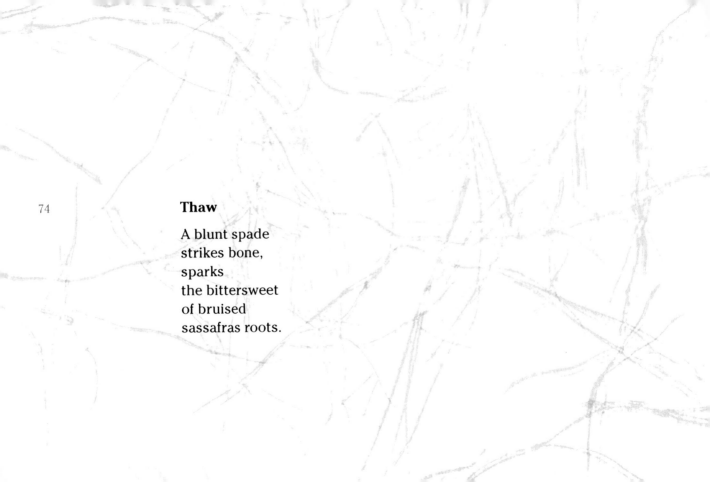

Thaw

A blunt spade
strikes bone,
sparks
the bittersweet
of bruised
sassafras roots.

Willow

The wounded
willow leans
over the riverbank
stirring
reflection
with its broken
branch.

Spring

Threads
its jagged hook
through my budding
backbone—
violent squalling.

Smile

That tired smile
again—
a pink
dogwood blossom
wilting
on the windowsill.

Puddle

Standing water
looks me
in the eye
so long
I see
clear through
my self.

Barrel

By midnight
primrose
and blossoming
apple tree,
the trash barrel
fumes.

Fledgling

Why do you
flutter
around
on the ground
when you know
you can
fly?

Mole

Armies of red
ants march
to feast
on the acres
plowed out
of your heart.

Dusk

He finished sowing
his silver queen
with blue spruce
shadows
on his boots.

Old Timer

Whittling corn-
flowers from water
maple twigs
in samara rain.

Swarm

Rain
and rising mist
when he shakes
bees
from their bustling
limb.

Peonies

What do
honeybees
and black ants
discuss
inside drooping
peonies?

Rhododendron

Your bright
trumpets buzz
in the steepest shade—
please teach me
your evergreen.

Butterfly

Weighing
shimmery
scales on
my fingertips—
free wings
fluttering.

Snapping Turtle

What is an ocean?
I'm just a snapping turtle.
It's hard to let go.

Dogs

Bolting
alongside, nipping
at the balding
tires' skull-bucking
shimmer.

Truck

Dragged
behind backfiring
days
by the wrists,
begging for more
time.

Casket

Sour smell
of dying
flowers filling
the living
room—
close this
evening.

Telling The Bees

The service is today.
They're fighting
over the flowers.
Fly, fly away!

Grackles

Convening
at the corners
of my eyes
to confirm
this life
sentence.

Widow

Wandering
fence lines
limp
as a morning
glory's spent
petals.

Tadpole

When you're stuck
in a rut,
everything depends
on the weather.

Dry Spell

Soft sighs
of bean sprouts
snapping
their necks
straining
to pierce
the scabbed
earth.

Callus

Summers
squandered
marching
barefoot
across plots
of sun-spurred
stones.

Cowshed

On moonless nights,
salt blocks are grinning
skulls in the abandoned
cowshed.

Windfalls

Overripe
silences
no body
can stomach—
waiting
for worms.

Barn

Warped
stall doors creak
on frayed hay string
hinges as bright
motes of dust swirl
between sinking
beams streaking
the empty loft.

Grandma

What's left of her
paces
the sagging porch
wearing
one sock,
crying for the dogs.

Hummingbird

Haunted
by the sound
of a ruby throat
shattering
against
reflection.

Daddy Longlegs

I'm tired
of asking
you where
the cattle
have gone—
stop pointing
at me.

Lure

A full moon
skims midnight—
burble and splash
of the overflowing
pond.

Stalks

Crushed
cornstalks jut
from puddles
livid
with drowning
crickets.

Home

Dancing
through barbed wire
just so I can feel
these fields
remember
my feet.

Acknowledgments

Grateful acknowledgment goes to the editors of the journals and publications where the poems in this collection were first published:

Across the Margin

Anthology of Appalachian Writers

Cleaver Magazine

Clockwise Cat

Cold Mountain Review

Fluent Magazine

Fried Chicken and Coffee

Gargoyle

Gloom Cupboard

Grab-A-Nickel

Hamilton Stone Review

Kestrel

Lux

Mad Hatters' Review

Maudlin House

SpeciaL THaNKS

Special thanks to the people who have supported this project through their unwavering kindness, feedback, and encouragement:

Árni Blandon	Helen Vitoria	Maggie Anderson
Bill Pifer	Helene Kalkvik	Marc Harshman
Chris Sturm	John Taylor	Marc Vincenz
Deniz Ataman	Kinna Poulsen	Marjun Arge Simonsen
Doug Van Gundy	Lee Sharkey	Mark Brazaitis

Melissa Bannister

Meredith Sue Willis

Mildred Stanley

Nancy McKeithen

Natalie Sypolt

Óli Jákup Niclasen

Patrick J. Stevens

Peter Munro

Phyllis Wilson Moore

Robert L. Ward

Sally Ebeling

Sigmund Myklevoll

Sylvia B. Shurbutt

Terry McNemar

Wilma Acree

Creative Team

Kendall Markley is a graphic designer from Sunbury, Ohio. She is the leader of ThinkDesign, a student-run design agency that promotes interdisciplinary collaborations among Ohio University's students and faculty. While pursuing her BFA in Graphic Design, Markley experiments with methods that allow her to organically synthesize analog and digital media.

Chris Sturm is an artist and illustrator from Parkersburg, West Virginia. She studied drawing and painting at The Ohio State University and has exhibited her work at a variety of locales. Sturm's artwork has recently appeared in the *Women of Appalachia* exhibition, and she is now busy preparing her solo exhibition, *The Human Spectacle*. On *Planet Chroma*, Sturm imparts her hard-won knowledge and experience to fellow painters. Learn more about the artist and her work at planetchroma.chris-sturm.com and chris-sturm.com.

MadHat Press

Formed in 2012 by Carol Novack and Marc Vincenz, MadHat Press is the publishing division of the literary nonprofit organization, MadHat, Inc. MadHat Press publishes poetry, fiction, nonfiction, critical theory, anthologies, and hybrid work. They champion the vital work of writers whose explosive, lyrical, passionate, deeply wrought voices push the boundaries of language, narrative, and image. For more information about the press and a list of available titles, visit madhat-press.com.

Praise

"*Whipstitches* is, like the author who so carefully penned these little gems of insight and poetic thoughtfulness, utterly unique and genuine. The poems in the volume are wonderfully terse, sparse, and packed with profundity. Sometimes humorous and wry, often quietly thoughtful, Randi Ward's poetry always leaves the reader thinking about the words and images long after the pages of her book have been closed. This kind of poetry is for all who appreciate a thoughtful moment and a small spot of time to carry with them throughout the day.

— Dr. Sylvia Bailey Shurbutt, managing editor of the *Anthology of Appalachian Writers*

"Each poem in *Whipstitches* is a world Ward makes us see, or see again, with a child's clarity melded to metaphor. Underlying the whole is both abiding love for the homeplace and knowledge of the wounds it inflicts."

— Lee Sharkey, author of *Calendars of Fire* and senior co-editor of *Beloit Poetry Journal*

"Randi Ward's poems: western-world haikus? In one sense they are, but these succinct, precisely crafted poems rarely conclude in a mere acknowledgment of the thing per se, the event per se, as in the Japanese literary genre. Ward's poems unfold unaffectedly, yet with increasing enigma. Snow is rarely just snow, broomsedge is rarely just broomsedge. *Whipstitches* narrates a subjectivity, a human body within the world, a poetic sensibility that is among the subtlest that I have encountered in my recent reading."

— John Taylor, author of *If Night is Falling* and *The Apocalypse Tapestries*

"The poems in *Whipstitches* are exquisite—keenly observed, delicately rendered moments that offer both beauty and wisdom. They show us what we think we know and leave us awed at what we've missed."

— Mark Brazaitis, author of *The Incurables* and *The Other Language*

THE AUTHOR

Randi Ward is a poet, translator, lyricist, and photographer from Belleville, West Virginia. She completed her undergraduate degree at Ohio University and subsequently earned her MA in Cultural Studies from the University of the Faroe Islands.

In 2013, Ward won the American-Scandinavian Foundation's Nadia Christensen Prize for her translation of Tóroddur Poulsen's *Fjalir* (*Planks*, 2013). This marked the first time in the international translation competition's history that a work of literature translated from the Faroese was awarded the prize.

Whipstitches is Ward's second collection of poetry. Her photography and writing have also appeared in *Asymptote, Beloit Poetry Journal, Cimarron Review, Vencil: Anthology of Contemporary Faroese Literature, World Literature Today,* and other publications.

Cornell University Library established the Randi Ward Collection in its Division of Rare and Manuscript Collections in 2015. For more information about the author and her work, visit randiward.com.

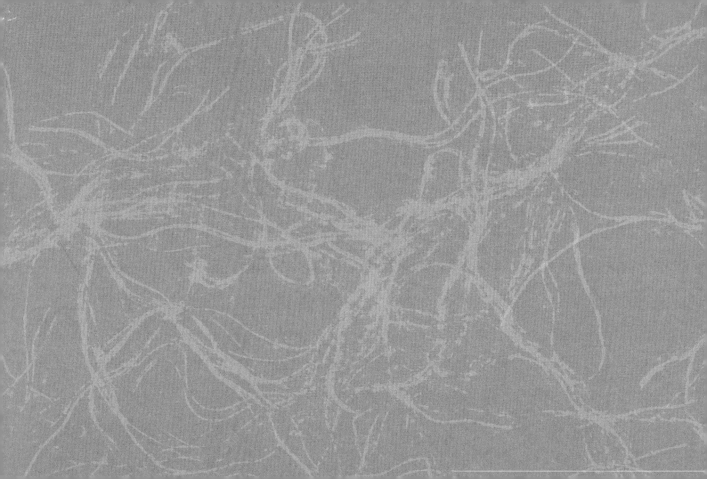